The Color of Islamophobia

Examining the Intersection of Racism and Anti-Muslim Prejudice

Larisa Vedzizhev

Table Of Content

Introduction

Islamophobia is a growing concern in America, as negative attitudes towards Muslims continue to pervade our society. From media portrayals to government policies, Muslims face a range of challenges and biases that can impact their daily lives. However, what is often overlooked in discussions of Islamophobia is the impact of race and ethnicity on the experience of discrimination.

"The Color of Islamophobia" is a book that seeks to explore the intersection of racism and anti-Muslim prejudice in America. By examining the ways in which race and ethnicity shape perceptions of Muslim identity, this book provides a powerful analysis of the challenges facing Muslim communities today. From profiling and discrimination to hate crimes and systemic bias, the authors offer a comprehensive examination of the complex ways in which race and Islamophobia intersect.

In this book, we will provide a historical context for anti-Muslim prejudice in America and explore the impact of media portrayals on public attitudes towards Muslims. We will also examine the ways in which government policies, such as the Muslim Ban and surveillance programs, have targeted Muslim communities and perpetuated Islamophobia.

However, the focus of this book is on the impact of race and ethnicity on the experience of Islamophobia. We will explore examples of anti-Muslim prejudice against Black, Latinx, and Asian Muslim communities, and how the intersection of race and religion shapes perceptions of Muslim identity.

We will also examine the impact of Islamophobia on Muslim communities, both in terms of the psychological impact on individuals and the ways in which discrimination reinforces systemic inequalities. We will provide strategies for resilience and community building in the face of discrimination, as well as examples of successful advocacy and activism against Islamophobia.

Finally, we will conclude by summarizing the key points of the book and reflecting on the importance of understanding the intersection of racism and Islamophobia in America. We hope that "The Color of Islamophobia" will inspire readers to confront their own biases and work towards a more just and inclusive society for all.

Definition of Islamophobia

Islamophobia is a multifaceted phenomenon characterized by an irrational fear, hostility, or prejudice towards Islam, Muslims, and Islamic culture. It encompasses a range of discriminatory attitudes and behaviors that negatively impact individuals and communities practicing or associated with the Islamic faith.

At its core, Islamophobia reflects an oversimplification and misrepresentation of Islam, often perpetuated by misconceptions, stereotypes, and biased narratives. This distorted understanding of Islam and its followers can lead to a climate of fear, suspicion, and intolerance.

Islamophobia manifests in various forms, including verbal abuse, physical attacks, discrimination in employment, housing, and education, as well as the enactment of policies targeting Muslim communities. It can also be observed through systemic biases, such as racial profiling, surveillance programs, and disproportionate scrutiny by law enforcement agencies.

The media plays a significant role in shaping public perceptions of Islam and Muslims. Sensationalized reporting, selective coverage, and the amplification of negative incidents can reinforce existing prejudices and contribute to the stigmatization of Muslims. This biased portrayal can perpetuate stereotypes, further marginalizing and isolating Muslim individuals and communities.

It is crucial to understand that Islamophobia does not solely target religious beliefs but also intersects with racial and ethnic identities. The experiences of Muslims vary depending on their racial or ethnic background, with individuals from Black, Latinx, or Asian Muslim communities often facing additional layers of discrimination due to the intersection of racism and Islamophobia.

The impact of Islamophobia extends beyond the individuals directly affected, as it undermines the principles of inclusivity, social cohesion, and religious freedom within a society. It fosters an environment of exclusion, hampers interfaith dialogue, and erodes the shared values of respect and understanding.

Recognizing and addressing Islamophobia requires a collective effort. Promoting education and awareness about Islam and Muslims, challenging stereotypes through accurate representation, and fostering intercultural dialogue are essential steps towards countering Islamophobia. Advocacy for policies that safeguard the rights and well-being of Muslim individuals and communities is also crucial in creating a more inclusive and equitable society.

By comprehensively understanding and actively working to dismantle Islamophobia, individuals, communities, and institutions can foster a climate of respect, empathy, and acceptance, ultimately building a more harmonious and diverse society for all.

Historical context of anti-Muslim prejudice in America

The history of anti-Muslim prejudice in America dates back to the earliest days of the country's founding. Even before the establishment of the United States, the Muslim faith was viewed with suspicion and hostility by European colonizers. In the 16th century, Spanish colonizers targeted Muslims in their campaigns of forced conversion and expulsion from Spain.

In the United States, anti-Muslim prejudice can be traced back to the colonial era. Muslim slaves were brought to the Americas as part of the transatlantic slave trade, and their Islamic beliefs were often suppressed by slaveholders. However, some enslaved Muslims were able to maintain their religious practices despite the harsh conditions of slavery.

In the late 19th century, with the influx of immigrants from the Middle East, anti-Muslim sentiment became more widespread. The Orientalist movement, which sought to define and categorize non-Western cultures, contributed to the negative portrayal of Islam and Muslims in the media and popular culture. In this period, Islam was often depicted as a backward, primitive, and violent religion.

The 20th century saw a resurgence of anti-Muslim prejudice in America, particularly after the Iranian Revolution of 1979. The American hostage crisis in Tehran, where US embassy personnel were held captive for over a year, fueled anti-Muslim sentiment in the US. Following the 9/11 terrorist attacks in 2001, there was a sharp rise in anti-Muslim hate crimes and discrimination in the US.

In recent years, there has been an increased recognition of the impact of Islamophobia on Muslim communities in America. Muslim individuals and organizations have advocated for their rights and raised awareness about the negative consequences of anti-Muslim prejudice. The public discourse has also shifted towards acknowledging and condemning Islamophobia, with prominent figures and organizations speaking out against discrimination and hate crimes targeting Muslims.

Despite these positive developments, anti-Muslim prejudice persists in various forms. Muslims are still subjected to discrimination in employment, housing, education, and other areas of life. Hate crimes targeting Muslims remain a significant concern, with a rise in such incidents in recent years. Additionally, policies targeting Muslims, such as travel bans and surveillance programs, continue to be enacted, despite their detrimental impact on the community.

Efforts to combat Islamophobia require a comprehensive approach that addresses its root causes and its impact on individuals and communities. Education and awareness-raising initiatives are crucial in promoting understanding and challenging stereotypes about Islam and Muslims. Advocacy for policies that safeguard the rights and well-being of Muslim individuals and communities is essential in ensuring equal treatment and protection under the law. Engaging in interfaith dialogue and building bridges of understanding between communities is also crucial in fostering social cohesion and promoting inclusivity.

Today, anti-Muslim prejudice remains a persistent issue in America, fueled by misinformation, stereotypes, and fear-mongering. Muslim communities continue to face discrimination, hate crimes, and systemic biases that undermine their rights and well-being. However, there has also been a growing movement of activists, scholars, and allies working to promote understanding and counter Islamophobia, recognizing the importance of building a more inclusive and equitable society for all.

Overview of the intersection of racism and Islamophobia

The intersection of racism and Islamophobia is a complex and multifaceted issue that involves the ways in which anti-Muslim prejudice intersects with other forms of discrimination, particularly racism. At its core, racism and Islamophobia share a common foundation: the dehumanization and stereotyping of a particular group of people based on their perceived racial, ethnic, or religious identity.

In the context of the US, racism and Islamophobia intersect in various ways. For example, many Muslim individuals and communities in the US are people of color, and they face not only discrimination based on their religious identity but also racism and xenophobia due to their race or ethnicity. This intersectional discrimination often manifests in various areas of life, such as employment, housing, education, and the criminal justice system.

Another way in which racism and Islamophobia intersect is through the impact of national security policies and initiatives. The US government's post-9/11 response to terrorism has disproportionately targeted Muslims, particularly those from Middle Eastern and South Asian countries. These policies, such as the travel ban and the Muslim registry, not only violate the civil rights of Muslim individuals but also reinforce and legitimize anti-Muslim stereotypes and xenophobia.

The intersection of racism and Islamophobia also plays out in the media and popular culture. Muslims, particularly those who are people of color, are often portrayed in the media as terrorists or violent extremists. This reinforces the negative stereotypes and dehumanization of Muslims, particularly those who are from countries with a history of colonialism and imperialism.

The intersection of racism and Islamophobia underscores the importance of addressing discrimination and prejudice in an intersectional and holistic manner. Efforts to combat Islamophobia must take into account the ways in which Muslim communities face intersecting forms of discrimination and work towards promoting equity and justice for all marginalized groups. This requires recognizing the interconnectedness of different forms of discrimination and the importance of building alliances across different communities to create a more inclusive and equitable society for all.

Chapter 1: The Roots of Islamophobia in America

Impact of 9/11 on American attitudes towards Muslims

The impact of the September 11, 2001 terrorist attacks on American attitudes towards Muslims cannot be overstated. The coordinated attacks on the World Trade Center and the Pentagon shook the nation to its core, leading to a wave of fear, anger, and grief. In the aftermath of 9/11, a significant shift occurred in the way many Americans viewed Islam and Muslims, creating a fertile ground for the growth of Islamophobia.

One of the immediate consequences of 9/11 was the association of the attacks with Islam as a whole. The hijackers' identification as Muslims led to a perception that Islam itself was responsible for the horrific acts of terrorism. This association fueled negative stereotypes, generalizations, and prejudice against Muslims, painting them as potential threats to national security.

The media played a crucial role in shaping public opinion in the aftermath of 9/11. Sensationalized reporting, fueled by fear and a thirst for answers, often perpetuated stereotypes about Muslims as violent extremists. News coverage frequently emphasized the religious affiliation of the attackers, contributing to the perception that Islam and terrorism were intrinsically linked. This biased representation of Muslims in the media further solidified existing prejudices and stigmatized the entire Muslim community.

Government policies enacted after 9/11 also had a significant impact on American attitudes towards Muslims. The passing of the USA PATRIOT Act and the establishment of programs such as the National Security Entry-Exit Registration System (NSEERS) resulted in increased surveillance, racial profiling, and targeting of Muslim individuals and communities. These policies created an atmosphere of suspicion and distrust, further exacerbating Islamophobia.

In the years following 9/11, hate crimes against Muslims soared, mosques were vandalized, and Muslims faced increased discrimination in various aspects of their lives, including employment, education, and housing. The rise of Islamophobia not only impacted the social and psychological well-being of Muslim individuals and communities but also reinforced systemic inequalities.

It is important to note that not all Americans responded to 9/11 with Islamophobia. Many individuals and organizations stood up against discrimination, actively worked to foster understanding, and advocated for the rights of Muslims. However, the overall impact of 9/11 on American attitudes towards Muslims cannot be ignored, as it contributed to the growth of Islamophobia and the perpetuation of stereotypes and prejudices that continue to affect Muslim communities in the United States to this day.

The role of media in perpetuating negative stereotypes

The role of media in perpetuating negative stereotypes cannot be understated when discussing Islamophobia. Media outlets, including television, film, print, and online platforms, have played a significant role in shaping public perceptions and attitudes towards Muslims.

One of the primary ways in which media perpetuates negative stereotypes is through sensationalized and biased reporting. After 9/11, there was a surge in media coverage focused on acts of terrorism committed by individuals claiming to be Muslims. These incidents received extensive coverage, leading to the perception that Muslims were inherently prone to violence and extremism. This kind of selective reporting creates a distorted picture of reality and reinforces the idea that Islam is a religion synonymous with terrorism.

Another factor contributing to negative stereotypes is the lack of nuanced and accurate portrayal of Muslims in media representation. Muslims are often portrayed as one-dimensional characters, limited to stereotypes such as terrorists, oppressed women, or foreign invaders. These limited portrayals fail to capture the diversity and complexity of Muslim individuals and communities, perpetuating a monolithic and dehumanizing narrative.

Additionally, the language used by media outlets in reporting on Islam and Muslims can contribute to bias and prejudice. Terms like "Islamic terrorism" or "radical Islam" link the entire religion of Islam with acts of violence, further stigmatizing and marginalizing Muslims. Such language reinforces the perception that Islam is inherently dangerous or incompatible with Western values, fostering an environment conducive to Islamophobia.

Furthermore, the frequency of media coverage of negative events involving Muslims far outweighs the coverage of positive contributions or stories that humanize Muslims. This imbalance creates a skewed representation of reality, leading to an overemphasis on negative experiences and reinforcing stereotypes.

Social media and online platforms have also played a significant role in perpetuating negative stereotypes. The rapid spread of misinformation, fake news, and Islamophobic content on these platforms can amplify biases and contribute to the dissemination of harmful stereotypes and prejudices.

It is crucial to recognize the responsibility that media outlets have in shaping public opinion. By promoting fair and accurate reporting, diversifying narratives, and challenging stereotypes, media can play a transformative role in countering Islamophobia. Ethical and responsible journalism can help break down barriers, foster understanding, and contribute to a more inclusive and tolerant society.

Historical examples of anti-Muslim bias in American history

Anti-Muslim bias in America has a long and complex history that can be traced back to the country's earliest days. Here are some historical examples of anti-Muslim bias in American history:

1. Slavery and the transatlantic slave trade: While slavery in America primarily affected African Americans, there were also Muslim slaves who were brought to the United States from Africa during the transatlantic slave

trade. These Muslim slaves faced discrimination, oppression, and forced conversion to Christianity.

2. Orientalism and Exclusion Acts: In the late 19th and early 20th centuries, American society was influenced by the Orientalist movement, which portrayed the Middle East and Asia as exotic and dangerous. This cultural bias contributed to the passage of the Chinese Exclusion Act of 1882 and the Immigration Act of 1924, which targeted Asian immigrants and also impacted Muslim immigrants from countries such as Turkey and Syria.

3. The Nation of Islam: The Nation of Islam was a Black nationalist and

religious movement founded in Detroit in 1930. The movement's teachings, which included a belief in a separate Black nation and the superiority of Black people, were seen by some as a threat to American society. The Nation of Islam and its leader, Elijah Muhammad, faced significant opposition and surveillance by the federal government.

4. The Iranian Hostage Crisis: In 1979, a group of Iranian students seized the US Embassy in Tehran and held 52 Americans hostage for 444 days. The crisis led to a surge of anti-Iranian sentiment in America, which also impacted Muslim individuals and communities. Iranian Americans faced

increased discrimination and violence, and mosques were vandalized and attacked.

5. Post-9/11 Islamophobia: The terrorist attacks on September 11, 2001, led to a surge in anti-Muslim sentiment in America. Muslims faced increased discrimination and violence, mosques were vandalized, and individuals were targeted due to their religious affiliation. Government policies such as the USA PATRIOT Act and the National Security Entry-Exit Registration System (NSEERS) reinforced Islamophobic attitudes and practices.

6. War on Terror: In the aftermath of 9/11, the United States launched the War on Terror, which included military operations in Afghanistan and Iraq. The wars contributed to the perception that Islam and Muslims were inherently violent and posed a threat to American security. The government's rhetoric and policies, including the use of torture and targeted killings, reinforced Islamophobic attitudes and practices.

7. Anti-Sharia Laws: In recent years, several states have introduced legislation aimed at prohibiting the use of Sharia (Islamic law) in American courts. These laws contribute to the perception that Muslims are a threat to American values and reinforce the idea

that Islam is incompatible with American democracy.

8. Muslim Ban: In 2017, President Donald Trump signed an executive order banning travel from several Muslim-majority countries. The ban was widely criticized as discriminatory and Islamophobic, and it contributed to the perception that Muslims were a threat to American security.

9. Hate Crimes: Hate crimes against Muslims have increased in recent years, with mosques and Muslim individuals facing vandalism, harassment, and violence. The FBI's Hate Crime Statistics report showed a

17% increase in hate crimes against Muslims in 2017.

10.   Political Rhetoric: Political rhetoric, particularly during election cycles, has contributed to the normalization of Islamophobia in American society. Candidates and elected officials have used anti-Muslim rhetoric to appeal to their base, reinforcing stereotypes and contributing to the marginalization of Muslim individuals and communities.

These historical examples demonstrate that anti-Muslim bias has been a persistent feature of American society. They also highlight the intersectionality of Islamophobia with other forms of oppression, such as racism, xenophobia, and imperialism. Recognizing and challenging this history is crucial to building a more inclusive and just society.

Chapter 2: The Color of Islamophobia

The impact of race and ethnicity on the experience of Islamophobia

The experience of Islamophobia is not uniform across all individuals who identify as Muslim, as the impact of race and ethnicity can significantly shape one's experience of discrimination and prejudice. Here are some ways in which race and ethnicity intersect with Islamophobia:

1. Black Muslims: Black Muslims in America face a unique form of Islamophobia that is often linked to anti-Black racism. Black Muslims face discrimination from both non-Muslims

and other Muslims due to their race and religious affiliation. The Nation of Islam, a predominantly Black Muslim group, has faced particular scrutiny and suspicion from the American government.

2. Arab and South Asian Muslims: Arab and South Asian Muslims are often the targets of Islamophobic rhetoric and policies due to their perceived association with terrorism. Following 9/11, Arab and South Asian Muslims faced increased surveillance, profiling, and discrimination. Government policies such as the Muslim Ban have specifically targeted individuals from these regions.

3. Latinx Muslims: Latinx Muslims face a unique experience of Islamophobia that is shaped by their intersectional identities. Latinx Muslims may face discrimination from both their Latinx and Muslim communities, and they often struggle to reconcile their identities within a society that views them as "outsiders" in multiple ways.

4. Southeast Asian Muslims: Southeast Asian Muslims, particularly those from countries such as Indonesia and Malaysia, may face discrimination from other Muslims due to differences in religious practices and cultural traditions. They may also face discrimination from non-Muslims due

to their perceived foreignness and association with terrorism.

5. Converts to Islam: Converts to Islam may face a different form of Islamophobia than individuals who were born into Muslim families. Converts may be seen as "outsiders" to both their non-Muslim and Muslim communities and may face discrimination and isolation as a result.

6. Multiracial Muslim Families: Multiracial Muslim families face unique challenges and experiences of Islamophobia. Children may face discrimination and confusion about their identity, while parents may face additional scrutiny from non-Muslim

and Muslim communities alike due to their interracial and interfaith marriages.

7. Indigenous Muslims: Indigenous Muslims in America, such as Native American and Alaska Native Muslims, face a specific form of Islamophobia that is shaped by the history of colonization and ongoing marginalization of indigenous communities. Indigenous Muslims may face discrimination from both non-Muslim and Muslim communities due to their indigenous and Muslim identities.

8. Afro-Latinx Muslims: Afro-Latinx Muslims face a unique intersection of

anti-Black racism, anti-Latinx racism, and Islamophobia. They may experience discrimination from both their Black and Latinx communities, as well as from non-Muslims and other Muslims due to their multiple identities.

9. Muslim Women: Muslim women, particularly those who wear hijab or other religious dress, may face additional discrimination and harassment due to their gender and religious identity. Islamophobic rhetoric often portrays Muslim women as oppressed and in need of rescue, perpetuating harmful stereotypes and further marginalizing Muslim women.

10. Class and Education: Class and education can also shape one's experience of Islamophobia. Muslim individuals who are lower income or less educated may face additional barriers to employment, housing, and education due to discrimination and prejudice. They may also be more vulnerable to Islamophobic policies and rhetoric.

Understanding the intersection of race, ethnicity, and other identities with Islamophobia is essential for developing more inclusive and effective strategies for combating discrimination and prejudice against Muslim individuals and communities. It is important to recognize the unique challenges and experiences faced by different groups within the Muslim community and to work towards building a more just and equitable society for all.

Examples of anti-Muslim prejudice against Black, Latinx, and Asian Muslim communities

Anti-Muslim prejudice can manifest in different ways against Black, Latinx, and Asian Muslim communities. Here are some examples of such prejudice:

1. Black Muslim Communities:

- Black Muslims often face discrimination from both non-Muslim and other Muslim communities due to the intersection of racism and Islamophobia.

- They may experience racial profiling, increased surveillance, and disproportionate scrutiny in security settings.

- Negative stereotypes about Black people, such as being associated with crime or violence, can also intersect with Islamophobic perceptions and contribute to heightened prejudice.

2. Latinx Muslim Communities:

- Latinx Muslims may face a unique set of challenges due to the intersection of their Latinx and Muslim identities.

- They may encounter prejudice from their Latinx communities for converting to Islam, which can be seen as deviating from cultural or religious norms.

- Islamophobic attitudes towards Latinx Muslims can stem from xenophobic beliefs about immigration, stereotypes of Latinx individuals as "foreign" or "outsiders," and misconceptions about Islam.

3. Asian Muslim Communities:

- Asian Muslims may face discrimination based on both their ethnicity and religious affiliation.
- Negative stereotypes and perceptions about Asians, such as the "model minority" myth or perceptions of

foreignness, can intersect with Islamophobic biases.

- Following events like the 9/11 attacks, Asian Muslims, particularly those from countries like Pakistan, Afghanistan, or Bangladesh, have been subject to increased scrutiny, racial profiling, and Islamophobic sentiment.

4. Stereotyping and Cultural Misunderstandings:

- All three communities may face generalizations and stereotypes related to their religious practices, cultural traditions, or appearance.
- Stereotypes may include assumptions about their level of religiosity,

perceived cultural backwardness, or patriarchal gender roles.

- These stereotypes and misunderstandings can contribute to discrimination, exclusion, and the perpetuation of harmful narratives about these communities.

5. Discrimination in Employment:

- Muslim individuals, particularly those from Black, Latinx, and Asian communities, may experience discrimination in employment due to their religious or ethnic identity.
- This can include being passed over for job opportunities, experiencing harassment or microaggressions in the

workplace, or facing barriers to career advancement.

- Discrimination in employment can have long-term consequences for individuals' economic stability and overall well-being.

6. Islamophobia in Education:

- Muslim students may experience discrimination in schools, including bullying, harassment, and exclusion from extracurricular activities.
- Negative stereotypes and misconceptions about Islam can also be perpetuated in educational materials or curriculum, which can further marginalize Muslim students.

- Discrimination in education can negatively impact students' academic performance, mental health, and sense of belonging in the school community.

7. Xenophobic Policies and Rhetoric:

- Anti-Muslim prejudice can be reinforced by xenophobic policies and rhetoric, such as travel bans or immigration restrictions targeting predominantly Muslim countries.
- These policies can perpetuate harmful stereotypes about Muslim individuals and communities, and contribute to feelings of exclusion and discrimination.

- Xenophobic policies and rhetoric can also have broader implications for social cohesion and national security.

8. Interfaith Relations:

- Building positive relationships between Muslim communities and other faith communities is essential for combating anti-Muslim prejudice.
- Interfaith initiatives can promote understanding and respect between different religious groups and challenge harmful stereotypes and misconceptions.
- Interfaith dialogue and collaboration can also lead to more inclusive policies and initiatives that benefit all members of society.

Addressing these various forms of anti-Muslim prejudice requires a multifaceted approach that involves education, policy reform, community engagement, and interfaith dialogue. By understanding the specific experiences and challenges faced by different Muslim communities, we can work towards building a more equitable and accepting society for all.

The role of skin color and ethnic background in shaping perceptions of Muslim identity

Skin color and ethnic background play a significant role in shaping perceptions of Muslim identity. Here are some key points on how these factors influence the perception of Muslim individuals:

1. Racialized Islamophobia: Islamophobia is often racialized, meaning that it intersects with racism and biases based on skin color and ethnic background. Muslims who are perceived as having a Middle Eastern, South Asian, or African ethnic background, and therefore have darker skin, often face higher levels of discrimination and prejudice. The intersection of Islamophobia and racism can result in compounded forms of marginalization and targeted discrimination.

2. Stereotyping and Assumptions: People's perceptions of Muslim

individuals are often influenced by stereotypes and assumptions associated with their skin color and ethnic background. For example, Muslims with darker skin may be stereotyped as more "foreign," "dangerous," or "suspect" due to racist stereotypes prevalent in society. These stereotypes can lead to increased scrutiny, surveillance, and bias in various aspects of life, including employment, education, and public spaces.

3. Exoticization and Orientalism: Individuals with ethnic backgrounds that are perceived as "exotic" or "foreign" may be subjected to Orientalist narratives and perceptions. Orientalism portrays Muslims as

mysterious, backwards, or inherently different from Western norms. This exoticization can reinforce a sense of otherness and contribute to the dehumanization and marginalization of Muslim individuals.

4. Colorism within Muslim Communities: Colorism, or discrimination based on skin color within a specific racial or ethnic group, can also impact the experiences of Muslim individuals. Lighter-skinned Muslims may receive more acceptance or privilege within their own communities, while darker-skinned Muslims may face additional scrutiny or bias.

5. Intersectionality and Multiple Identities: Muslim individuals may have multiple identities based on their skin color, ethnic background, and other factors such as gender or socio-economic status. These intersecting identities can shape their experiences of discrimination and prejudice. For instance, Black Muslim women may face both anti-Black racism and gendered Islamophobia, while Asian Muslim individuals may navigate the intersection of anti-Asian racism and Islamophobia.

Understanding the role of skin color and ethnic background in shaping perceptions of Muslim identity is crucial for recognizing and challenging biases and stereotypes.

Promoting inclusivity, intersectional understanding, and anti-racist practices are essential steps toward creating a more equitable and accepting society for all Muslims, regardless of their skin color or ethnic background.

Chapter 3: Islamophobia and Systemic Bias

The impact of government policies on Muslim communities, including the Muslim Ban and surveillance programs
Government policies have had a profound impact on Muslim communities, particularly through the implementation of discriminatory measures such as the Muslim Ban and surveillance programs. Here are some key points on their impact:

1. Muslim Ban:

- The Muslim Ban, officially known as Executive Order 13769, was signed by President Donald Trump in 2017. It initially restricted entry into the United States for citizens of seven predominantly Muslim-majority countries, and later expanded to include additional countries.

- The Muslim Ban contributed to a sense of fear, anxiety, and uncertainty among Muslim communities. It reinforced negative stereotypes about Muslims, perpetuated Islamophobia, and sent a message that individuals from these countries were inherently suspicious or dangerous.

- Families were separated, students and professionals faced difficulties in pursuing educational and career opportunities, and individuals experienced emotional distress and discrimination as a result of the travel ban.

2. Surveillance Programs:

- Government surveillance programs, such as the National Security Agency's (NSA) bulk collection of phone and internet data, have disproportionately targeted Muslim communities.
- These programs have infringed upon the privacy rights of individuals, leading to a chilling effect on free speech, religious practices, and community organizing within Muslim communities.
- The perception of being under constant surveillance has fostered an atmosphere of mistrust, fear, and self-censorship

within Muslim communities, impacting their sense of belonging and ability to freely express their religious and cultural identities.

3. Profiling and Targeting:

- Government policies, such as the implementation of profiling practices by law enforcement agencies, have disproportionately targeted Muslim communities.

- Racial and religious profiling has resulted in increased scrutiny, harassment, and discrimination faced by Muslim individuals in various aspects of their lives, including travel, employment, and public spaces.

- These policies have contributed to a climate of fear, stigmatization, and marginalization within Muslim communities, undermining their sense of security and equal treatment under the law.

4. Impact on Mental Health and Well-being:

- The discriminatory nature of government policies has had significant psychological and emotional consequences on Muslim individuals and communities.
- The experiences of being targeted, surveilled, and stigmatized can lead to increased stress, anxiety, depression, and a sense of alienation.

- The impact on mental health can extend beyond individuals to affect the overall well-being of families and communities, straining social bonds and hindering community resilience.

Addressing the impact of these government policies requires advocating for the repeal or reform of discriminatory measures, challenging Islamophobic narratives, promoting community empowerment, and protecting civil liberties and human rights. It is essential to create an inclusive society that values the dignity, rights, and contributions of all individuals, regardless of their religious or ethnic background.

Discrimination in employment, housing, and education

Discrimination in employment, housing, and education continues to be a significant challenge faced by Muslim individuals and communities. Here's a breakdown of the discrimination experienced in each of these areas:

1. Employment Discrimination:

- Muslim individuals often face discrimination in the job market based on their religious identity.
- They may encounter barriers to equal employment opportunities, including being denied job interviews or

promotions, facing unequal pay, or experiencing workplace harassment.

- Discrimination in employment can also manifest as policies or practices that disproportionately affect Muslim employees, such as restrictions on religious attire or scheduling conflicts related to religious observances.

2. Housing Discrimination:

- Muslim individuals may experience discrimination when seeking housing or renting properties.
- They may face refusal of rental applications, discriminatory rental terms, or discriminatory treatment by landlords or housing providers.

- Discrimination in housing can also include harassment, eviction threats, or discriminatory practices based on religious attire, names, or ethnic backgrounds.

3. Education Discrimination:

- Muslim students often encounter discrimination and bias in educational settings.
- They may experience bullying, harassment, or exclusion based on their religious beliefs, cultural practices, or visible markers of their Muslim identity, such as wearing hijab.
- Schools may also fail to accommodate religious observances or provide an inclusive learning environment, which

can negatively impact Muslim students' educational experiences and well-being.

Addressing discrimination in employment, housing, and education requires concerted efforts from various stakeholders:

1. Legal Protections and Policies:

- Implementing and strengthening anti-discrimination laws and policies at the local, state, and national levels is crucial.
- Legal protections should explicitly prohibit discrimination based on religious identity and provide avenues for reporting and addressing discriminatory incidents.

2. Awareness and Sensitivity Training:

- Employers, housing providers, and educational institutions should provide training programs to raise awareness about religious diversity, cultural sensitivity, and the impact of discrimination.
- Training programs can promote inclusive practices, challenge biases, and foster respectful environments.

3. Community Engagement and Advocacy:

- Muslim communities can engage in advocacy efforts to raise awareness about discrimination and work towards policy changes.

- Building alliances with other marginalized communities and promoting interfaith dialogue can strengthen collective efforts to combat discrimination.

4. Educational Initiatives:

- Educational institutions should foster inclusive and multicultural learning environments that celebrate diversity and combat stereotypes.
- Implementing comprehensive anti-bullying policies, providing cultural and religious sensitivity training for teachers and staff, and promoting intercultural understanding

can contribute to more inclusive educational settings.

By addressing discrimination in employment, housing, and education, society can create equal opportunities, promote social cohesion, and ensure that all individuals, including Muslims, can fully participate and thrive in all aspects of life.

The intersection of Islamophobia and other forms of oppression, such as homophobia and transphobia

The intersection of Islamophobia with other forms of oppression, such as homophobia and transphobia, is a complex and multifaceted issue. Here are some key points to understand this intersection:

1. Marginalization within Muslim Communities:

- Muslim individuals who identify as LGBTQ+ may face unique challenges within Muslim communities due to the intersection of their religious and sexual or gender identities.
- Homophobia, transphobia, and stigma against LGBTQ+ individuals can exist within Muslim communities, leading to discrimination, exclusion, and even violence.
- LGBTQ+ Muslims may experience pressure to hide their sexual or gender identities, undergo conversion therapy,

or face rejection from their families and communities.

2. Islamophobic Perceptions of LGBTQ+ Muslims:

- Islamophobic narratives often reinforce negative stereotypes about Muslims and link them to homophobia or transphobia.
- Islamophobes may exploit the intersection of Islamophobia and LGBTQ+ rights to perpetuate negative portrayals of Islam and Muslims, painting them as inherently homophobic or transphobic.
- This can further marginalize LGBTQ+ Muslims, subjecting them to both

Islamophobic and homophobic/transphobic prejudice.

3. Safety and Well-being:

- The intersection of Islamophobia, homophobia, and transphobia can create unique safety concerns for LGBTQ+ Muslims.
- They may face a heightened risk of violence, hate crimes, or family and community rejection.
- These safety concerns can have a significant impact on their mental health, well-being, and ability to fully express their identities.

4. Advocacy and Support:

- Organizations and individuals working towards LGBTQ+ rights and social justice need to address the intersecting forms of oppression that LGBTQ+ Muslims face.

- It is important to foster inclusive spaces that embrace both religious and sexual or gender identities, providing support and resources for LGBTQ+ Muslims.

- Advocacy efforts should focus on challenging both Islamophobia and homophobia/transphobia, fostering dialogue, and promoting understanding between different communities.

Navigating the intersection of Islamophobia and homophobia/transphobia requires a nuanced and inclusive approach that acknowledges the diverse experiences and identities within Muslim communities. By promoting dialogue, understanding, and advocating for the rights and dignity of all individuals, we can work towards creating a more inclusive and accepting society that respects the rights and identities of LGBTQ+ Muslims.

Chapter 4: The Impact of Islamophobia on Muslim Communities

The psychological impact of Islamophobia on Muslim individuals and communities

Islamophobia has profound psychological impacts on Muslim individuals and communities. Here are some key points regarding the psychological consequences of Islamophobia:

1. Fear, Anxiety, and Hyper-Vigilance:

- Islamophobia creates a pervasive sense of fear and anxiety among Muslim individuals and communities.

- The constant threat of discrimination, harassment, or violence leads to a state of hyper-vigilance, where individuals are constantly on guard and anticipating potential Islamophobic incidents.

- This heightened sense of fear and anxiety can have detrimental effects on mental health and overall well-being.

2. Identity Crisis and Self-Esteem:

- Islamophobic attitudes and actions can contribute to an identity crisis for Muslim individuals.

- Constant negative portrayals, stereotypes, and dehumanizing narratives can lead to a struggle with self-acceptance and self-esteem.

- Muslim individuals may experience feelings of shame, self-doubt, and internalized Islamophobia, which can significantly impact their psychological well-being.

3. Psychological Distress and Trauma:

- Islamophobia can cause psychological distress and trauma, especially when individuals or communities are targeted by hate crimes, verbal abuse, or physical violence.

- Direct experiences or witnessing Islamophobic incidents can result in symptoms of post-traumatic stress disorder (PTSD), anxiety disorders, depression, and other psychological disorders.

- The cumulative effect of ongoing Islamophobia can erode mental health resilience and lead to chronic psychological distress.

4. Social Isolation and Alienation:

- Islamophobia can create a sense of social isolation and alienation for Muslim individuals and communities.
- Fear of discrimination or negative reactions may lead to withdrawal from social interactions or reluctance to openly express one's Muslim identity.
- This social isolation can contribute to feelings of loneliness, depression, and a diminished sense of belonging.

5. Impact on Children and Youth:

- Islamophobia can have a significant impact on the mental health and well-being of Muslim children and youth.
- They may experience bullying, harassment, or exclusion at school, leading to feelings of fear, anxiety, and low self-esteem.
- These negative experiences during formative years can have long-lasting effects on their mental health and educational outcomes.

Addressing the psychological impact of Islamophobia requires concerted efforts from various stakeholders:

1. Education and Awareness:

- Promoting education and awareness about Islamophobia, its impact, and the experiences of Muslim individuals and communities can help challenge stereotypes and foster empathy.
- Schools, workplaces, and community organizations can implement programs that promote cultural sensitivity, inclusivity, and religious literacy.

2. Mental Health Support:

- Providing accessible and culturally sensitive mental health services that address the specific needs of Muslim individuals is crucial.
- Cultivating safe spaces and support networks where individuals can share

their experiences and find support is important for healing and resilience.

3. Empowerment and Advocacy:

- Empowering Muslim individuals and communities to counter Islamophobia by raising their voices, sharing their stories, and advocating for their rights is essential.
- Collaborating with allies and organizations dedicated to combating Islamophobia can help create systemic change and challenge discriminatory narratives.

By addressing the psychological impact of Islamophobia and fostering a climate of acceptance and inclusion, society can support the well-being and resilience of Muslim individuals and communities.

The ways in which Islamophobia reinforces systemic inequalities

Islamophobia reinforces systemic inequalities in a variety of ways, perpetuating discrimination and marginalization for Muslim individuals and communities. Here are some key points regarding how Islamophobia reinforces systemic inequalities:

1. Economic Inequality:

- Islamophobia can limit job opportunities, access to education, and housing options for Muslim individuals, contributing to economic inequality.

- Muslim individuals may face discriminatory hiring practices or limited career advancement due to their religion or ethnicity.
- Islamophobic attitudes and actions can also lead to exclusion from economic opportunities or resources, such as loans or grants.

2. Legal and Political Inequality:

- Islamophobic policies, such as the Muslim Ban or surveillance programs, reinforce legal and political inequalities for Muslim individuals and communities.

- These policies contribute to the perception of Muslim individuals as outsiders or potential threats, leading to exclusion from legal protections or political participation.
- The stigmatization of Muslim individuals as "other" reinforces the unequal distribution of power and resources in society.

3. Social and Cultural Inequality:

- Islamophobia perpetuates social and cultural inequalities by reinforcing negative stereotypes and limiting opportunities for cultural expression and integration.

- Muslim individuals may face exclusion or discrimination in social settings, such as in schools or neighborhoods.

- Islamophobic attitudes and actions can also limit access to cultural resources or opportunities, such as museums or community events.

4. Health Inequality:

- Islamophobia can contribute to health inequalities for Muslim individuals and communities.

- Negative attitudes towards Muslim individuals may lead to discrimination in healthcare settings or limited access to culturally sensitive healthcare.

- The stress and trauma of experiencing Islamophobia can also have negative health consequences, such as increased risk for chronic illnesses or mental health disorders.

5. Environmental Inequality:

- Islamophobia can reinforce environmental inequalities by perpetuating the exclusion of Muslim individuals and communities from environmental decision-making processes.
- Muslim communities may experience disproportionate exposure to environmental hazards or a lack of access to green spaces and healthy environments.
- The marginalization of Muslim individuals from environmental justice

initiatives perpetuates unequal distribution of environmental benefits and harms.

Addressing the ways in which Islamophobia reinforces systemic inequalities requires systemic change, advocacy, and allyship:

1. Advocacy:

- Advocating for policies that promote equity, such as anti-discrimination laws or inclusive hiring practices, can help reduce systemic inequalities for Muslim individuals and communities.
- Advocating for the rights of Muslim individuals in legal and political spheres can help counteract Islamophobic policies.

2. Allyship:

- Engaging in allyship with Muslim individuals and communities can help reduce systemic inequalities.
- Allies can support Muslim individuals in advocating for their rights and creating inclusive environments, such as schools or workplaces.
- Amplifying the voices of Muslim individuals in environmental justice initiatives can help promote equitable distribution of resources.

3. Education:

- Educating oneself and others about the ways in which Islamophobia reinforces systemic inequalities can help challenge stereotypes and foster empathy.

- Educating oneself on the experiences of Muslim individuals and communities can help identify and address systemic inequalities.

By addressing the ways in which Islamophobia reinforces systemic inequalities, society can promote equity and justice for Muslim individuals and communities.

Strategies for resilience and community building in the face of discrimination

Experiencing discrimination can take a toll on one's mental health and well-being, as well as the social and emotional health of their community. In the face of discrimination, building resilience and creating a sense of community can be helpful strategies. Here are some potential strategies for resilience and community building in the face of discrimination:

1. Seek Support:

- Building a support network of individuals who share similar experiences can be beneficial in promoting resilience.
- Seeking out therapy or counseling services can also be helpful in

processing experiences of discrimination.

2. Engage in Self-Care:

- Engaging in self-care practices, such as exercise or meditation, can help manage stress and promote emotional well-being.
- Taking breaks from social media or news outlets can also help reduce the negative impact of discrimination on one's mental health.

3. Connect with Community:

- Participating in community events or organizations that focus on promoting inclusivity and diversity can help create a sense of belonging and resilience.

- Building connections with individuals from diverse backgrounds can also promote a sense of community and understanding.

4. Educate Others:

- Educating others about discrimination and its impact can promote awareness and allyship.
- Sharing personal experiences can also help build empathy and understanding.

5. Advocate for Change:

- Advocating for policies or initiatives that promote inclusivity and equity can help address the root causes of discrimination.

- Engaging in political or social action can also promote resilience and a sense of agency in the face of discrimination.

6. Foster Resilience through Spirituality:

- For some, spirituality can be a source of strength and resilience in the face of discrimination.

- Engaging in spiritual practices, such as prayer or meditation, can help promote emotional well-being and a sense of community.

Overall, building resilience and creating a sense of community can be helpful strategies for coping with discrimination. By seeking support, engaging in self-care, connecting with community, educating others, advocating for change, and fostering resilience through spirituality, individuals and communities can work towards creating a more equitable and inclusive society.

Chapter 5: Confronting Islamophobia and Racism

Strategies for challenging Islamophobia and promoting diversity and inclusion

Challenging Islamophobia and promoting diversity and inclusion requires a collective effort. Here are some strategies that individuals and communities can employ to challenge Islamophobia and foster a more inclusive society:

1. Education and Awareness:

- Promote education and awareness about Islam and Muslim cultures to dispel stereotypes and misconceptions.

- Encourage dialogue and learning about Islamophobia, its impact, and the experiences of Muslim individuals and communities.
- Foster cross-cultural understanding by organizing workshops, seminars, or cultural exchange programs.

2. Counter Stereotypes and Myths:

- Challenge and confront Islamophobic stereotypes and myths whenever they arise.
- Share accurate information and personal stories to challenge misconceptions and promote understanding.
- Encourage media outlets to present diverse and accurate representations of

Muslims and challenge biased narratives.

3. Allyship and Solidarity:

- Stand in solidarity with Muslim individuals and communities by actively supporting their rights and advocating against discrimination.
- Foster relationships and alliances with diverse groups, including interfaith organizations and social justice movements, to build a united front against Islamophobia.

4. Promote Inclusive Spaces:

- Create inclusive spaces within educational institutions, workplaces, and communities where diverse voices and perspectives are respected and valued.

- Implement inclusive policies that accommodate religious practices, dress codes, and cultural traditions.

- Encourage diverse representation in decision-making processes and leadership positions.

5. Combat Hate Speech and Discrimination:

- Speak out against Islamophobic hate speech and discrimination, whether it occurs online, in public spaces, or in interpersonal interactions.

- Report incidents of Islamophobia to relevant authorities and organizations dedicated to combating discrimination.
- Support anti-discrimination laws and initiatives that protect the rights of Muslim individuals and communities.

6. Engage in Grassroots Activism:

- Get involved in grassroots activism and advocacy efforts focused on challenging Islamophobia and promoting diversity and inclusion.
- Join or support organizations that work towards social justice, civil rights, and equality for all individuals, regardless of their religious background.

7. Media Literacy:

- Develop media literacy skills to critically analyze and challenge biased portrayals of Islam and Muslims in media.

- Support and promote media outlets that provide accurate and inclusive coverage of Muslim communities.

- Engage in constructive conversations and fact-checking when encountering Islamophobic content online.

8. Empower Muslim Voices:

- Amplify the voices of Muslim individuals and communities by sharing their stories, experiences, and contributions.

- Support Muslim-led initiatives, organizations, and businesses to foster economic empowerment and representation.

9. Continuous Self-Reflection:

- Engage in continuous self-reflection to examine personal biases and stereotypes that may contribute to Islamophobia.
- Challenge one's own assumptions and actively seek to learn from diverse perspectives.

By employing these strategies, individuals and communities can actively challenge Islamophobia, promote diversity and inclusion, and contribute to creating a more equitable and just society.

The importance of allyship and solidarity in combating anti-Muslim bias

Allyship and solidarity play a crucial role in combating anti-Muslim bias and creating a more inclusive and equitable society. Here's why allyship and solidarity are important:

1. Amplifying Marginalized Voices: As an ally, you can use your privilege and platform to amplify the voices and experiences of marginalized Muslim individuals and communities. By sharing their stories and perspectives, you help challenge stereotypes and

misconceptions and promote a more nuanced understanding of Islam and Muslims.

2. Providing Support and Protection: Allies can provide support and protection to Muslim individuals facing discrimination or hate crimes. By standing up against Islamophobic acts and advocating for their rights, allies create safer spaces and send a powerful message that discrimination will not be tolerated.

3. Challenging Stereotypes and Prejudices: Allies have the power to challenge and confront stereotypes and prejudices about Islam and Muslims. By actively challenging

misconceptions, sharing accurate information, and engaging in respectful dialogue, allies help break down barriers and promote a more inclusive and informed society.

4. Learning and Unlearning: Allies have the opportunity to learn from Muslim individuals and communities. Engaging in conversations, attending workshops or events, and seeking to understand their experiences can help allies unlearn their own biases and develop a more empathetic and nuanced perspective.

5. Collaborative Advocacy: Allies can join forces with Muslim individuals and organizations to advocate for

policies and initiatives that combat anti-Muslim bias. By working together, allies and Muslim communities can strengthen their impact and create lasting change.

6. Building Coalitions: Allies can build coalitions with other marginalized communities and social justice movements. Recognizing the interconnectedness of different forms of oppression and working together can create a powerful collective voice against discrimination and injustice.

7. Shifting Social Norms: Through allyship and solidarity, allies have the potential to influence social norms and create a culture of inclusivity and

acceptance. By challenging discriminatory behaviors, language, and attitudes in their own circles, allies can create ripples of change that extend beyond their immediate impact.

8. Personal Growth and Self-Reflection: Engaging in allyship requires continuous self-reflection and personal growth. Allies must examine their own biases, confront their privileges, and actively seek to learn and unlearn. This process not only benefits the communities they support but also contributes to their own personal development.

In short, allyship and solidarity are essential in combating anti-Muslim bias. By amplifying marginalized voices, providing support, challenging stereotypes, learning and unlearning, collaborating in advocacy, building coalitions, shifting social norms, and engaging in personal growth, allies contribute to a more inclusive, empathetic, and equitable society for all.

Examples of successful advocacy and activism against Islamophobia

There have been numerous successful advocacy and activism efforts against Islamophobia, demonstrating the power of collective action and commitment to combating anti-Muslim bias. Here are some examples of successful advocacy and activism against Islamophobia:

1. Campaigns for Awareness and Education:

- The "I Am Not a Stereotype" campaign led by the Council on American-Islamic Relations (CAIR) aims to challenge stereotypes and misconceptions about Islam and Muslims through media campaigns, educational resources, and community outreach.

- The "Take on Hate" campaign, initiated by the National Network for Arab American Communities (NNAAC), works to challenge hate and discrimination against Arab Americans, including Muslims, through grassroots organizing, media engagement, and legislative advocacy.

2. Legal Advocacy:

- The American Civil Liberties Union (ACLU) has been involved in several successful legal battles against Islamophobic policies and practices. For example, they challenged the constitutionality of the Muslim Ban executive orders, resulting in legal victories and significant public awareness about the discriminatory impact of such policies.
- Muslim Advocates is an organization that utilizes legal advocacy to combat Islamophobia. They have achieved successes in challenging discriminatory

practices, such as advocating for the right of Muslim individuals to wear religious attire in various settings.

3. Interfaith Initiatives:

- The Shoulder to Shoulder campaign is an interfaith coalition that mobilizes religious leaders and organizations to stand in solidarity against anti-Muslim sentiment and to promote interfaith dialogue and understanding.
- The Sisterhood of Salaam Shalom brings together Jewish and Muslim women to build relationships, foster understanding, and challenge Islamophobia and anti-Semitism through dialogue, education, and joint advocacy efforts.

4. Community Organizing:

- The Arab American Association of New York (AAANY) engages in community organizing and empowerment initiatives to challenge Islamophobia and support Arab and Muslim communities. They provide social services, education programs, and advocacy efforts to address the needs and combat discrimination faced by these communities.

- The #OurThreeWinners campaign, initiated by the families of Deah Barakat, Yusor Abu-Salha, and Razan Abu-Salha who were murdered in a hate crime, works to challenge Islamophobia and other forms of bigotry by promoting dialogue, understanding, and community building.

5. Grassroots Activism:

- Muslim-led grassroots organizations such as MPower Change and CAIR chapters across the United States have been successful in mobilizing communities, conducting educational campaigns, and advocating for policies that combat Islamophobia.
- The Muslim Anti-Racism Collaborative (MuslimARC) works to address systemic racism and Islamophobia through research, training, and organizing efforts,

promoting dialogue and action towards justice and inclusion.

These examples illustrate the diverse range of successful advocacy and activism against Islamophobia. By raising awareness, engaging in legal battles, fostering interfaith relationships, organizing at the community level, and utilizing grassroots activism, these initiatives have made significant strides in challenging Islamophobia, promoting understanding, and fostering a more inclusive society.

Conclusion

Islamophobia and racism in America have been deeply ingrained in American history, and continue to be a persistent problem in our society today. The negative stereotypes and biases that persist against Muslim communities and individuals have far-reaching impacts, from discrimination in employment, housing, and education to surveillance and harassment by law enforcement.

However, the stories of resilience and activism against Islamophobia demonstrate that change is possible. Through advocacy efforts, legal battles, interfaith initiatives, community organizing, and grassroots activism, people across the country have challenged anti-Muslim sentiment and worked towards greater understanding and inclusion.

The intersectional nature of Islamophobia also highlights the importance of solidarity and allyship with other marginalized communities. By recognizing the ways in which Islamophobia reinforces systemic inequalities and working towards a more equitable society for all, we can create a more just and inclusive future.

As we move forward, it is important to continue learning and engaging with the experiences and perspectives of Muslim communities and individuals, and to remain committed to challenging Islamophobia in all its forms. Through collective action and a shared commitment to justice and equality, we can work towards a more inclusive and compassionate society.

Call to action for readers to work towards a more just and inclusive society

As we conclude this book, it is essential to reflect on the issues of Islamophobia and racism in America, and recognize the responsibility we all bear in working towards a more just and inclusive society. Each and every one of us has a role to play in challenging discrimination, dismantling stereotypes, and promoting equality. Here is a call to action for readers to actively engage in this important work:

1. Educate Yourself: Commit to ongoing learning about Islam, Muslim cultures, and the experiences of Muslim individuals and communities. Challenge your own biases and misconceptions, and seek out diverse sources of information to develop a more nuanced understanding.

2. Speak Out: Do not remain silent in the face of Islamophobic or racist comments, jokes, or acts. Use your voice to challenge bigotry, stereotypes, and discrimination. Engage in respectful and constructive conversations to promote understanding and empathy.

3. Be an Ally: Stand in solidarity with Muslim individuals and communities. Listen to their stories, amplify their voices, and support their rights. Learn from and engage with diverse communities to build bridges and foster unity.

4. Advocate for Change: Get involved in advocacy efforts to combat Islamophobia and racism. Support organizations and initiatives that work towards social justice and equality. Use your influence and resources to advocate for inclusive policies and practices in your workplace, educational institutions, and communities.

5. Foster Inclusive Spaces: Create environments that embrace diversity and inclusion. Challenge systemic biases and promote equitable practices in employment, housing, and education. Encourage dialogue and interfaith understanding to build bridges between different communities.

6. Engage in Community Building: Participate in community organizations and initiatives that promote inclusivity and social cohesion. Foster relationships with individuals from diverse backgrounds and actively seek to understand their experiences and perspectives.

7. Vote and Engage Politically: Support political candidates and initiatives that prioritize equality, justice, and the rights of marginalized communities. Exercise your right to vote and engage in political processes to shape policies and institutions that challenge Islamophobia and racism.

8. Practice Empathy and Solidarity: Cultivate empathy and understanding by actively listening to the experiences of others. Stand in solidarity with not only Muslim individuals and communities but also other marginalized groups facing discrimination. Recognize the interconnectedness of different forms

of oppression and work towards collective liberation.

By taking these actions, we can contribute to a society where diversity is celebrated, where everyone can live free from discrimination and prejudice. The journey towards a more just and inclusive society requires collective effort, and it starts with each one of us. Together, let us challenge Islamophobia, racism, and all forms of discrimination, and create a future where everyone is valued, respected, and embraced for who they are.

Reflection on the importance of understanding the intersection of racism and Islamophobia in America

Reflecting on the importance of understanding the intersection of racism and

Islamophobia in America, it becomes evident that these two forms of discrimination are intertwined and cannot be addressed in isolation. Muslims in America, particularly those who are Black, Latinx, or Asian, face not only religious bias but also racial prejudice. Understanding the complex ways in which these forms of discrimination intersect is crucial for building a more just and inclusive society.

One of the key reasons why it is important to understand the intersection of racism and Islamophobia is that it sheds light on the experiences of Muslim individuals and communities. Discrimination against Muslims is not only driven by religious bias but also by the ways in which their identities intersect with their race, ethnicity, and national origin. For example, Muslim individuals who are Black or Latinx may face additional discrimination due to their skin color or immigrant status, while Asian Muslims may experience xenophobic sentiments due to their ethnic background.

Furthermore, recognizing the intersection of racism and Islamophobia also highlights the systemic nature of these forms of discrimination. Discrimination against Muslims is not simply the result of individual bias, but also reflects broader structural inequalities in American society. Understanding this intersection can lead to a deeper analysis of how institutionalized racism and Islamophobia are perpetuated and how they can be dismantled.

Finally, understanding the intersection of racism and Islamophobia is also essential for building alliances across different communities. Recognizing the ways in which different forms of oppression intersect can foster solidarity and empathy between groups facing different forms of discrimination. It can also promote collaboration and advocacy efforts to challenge systemic discrimination and promote equality.

In conclusion, understanding the intersection of racism and Islamophobia is critical for addressing discrimination against Muslims in America. By recognizing the complex ways in which these forms of discrimination intersect, we can work towards building a more just and inclusive society that values diversity and promotes equality for all.

www.ingramcontent.com/pod-product-compliance
Lightning Source LLC
Chambersburg PA
CBHW061354250726
48657CB00004B/1484